The Crash of
The
Concorde

AIR FRANCE

Ann Byers

the rosen publishing group's
rosen central

To Lloyd Wells, who gave my children their first airplane rides

Published in 2003 by The Rosen Publishing Group, Inc.
29 East 21st Street, New York, NY 10010

First Edition

Library of Congress Cataloging-in-Publication Data

Byers, Ann.
The crash of the Concorde / Ann Byers. — 1st ed.
p. cm. — (When disaster strikes!)
Summary: Recounts the crash of the Concorde in 2000, events leading up to the tragedy, the investigation that followed, and ramifications of the first fatal accident involving this supersonic passenger jet.
Includes bibliographical references and index.
ISBN 0-8239-3673-2 (library binding)
1. Aircraft accidents—France—Paris—Juvenile literature. 2. Concorde (Jet transports)—Juvenile literature. [1. Aircraft accidents. 2. Concorde (Jet transports) 3. Jet planes.]
I. Title. II. When disaster strikes! (New York, N.Y.)
TL553.53.F8 B95 2003
363.12'492—dc21

2001008526

Manufactured in the United States of America

On the cover:
An Air France Concorde lands at a military base in southern France on January 18, 2001. The flight was only the second by a Concorde after the July 2000 crash.

Contents

French firemen douse the smoldering wreckage after the July 25, 2000, crash of an Air France Concorde.

Introduction

On July 25, 2000, an Air France Concorde jet streaked across the sky trailing flames. Only two minutes after takeoff, it crashed a few miles outside of Paris. With the 113 people killed in the crash, the dream of supersonic travel also seemed to die.

A century earlier, supersonic travel—flying faster than the speed of sound—seemed an impossible dream. After all, a weeklong crossing of the Atlantic in a steamer was considered a rapid form of transportation. Yet by midcentury, the dream of commercial supersonic travel—air travel for paying customers—was becoming a reality, and in 1969 the Concorde became the first passenger plane to break the sound barrier. Two years later, it crossed the Atlantic in less than four hours. A brave new world of air travel had been born.

A Dream Is Born

The Concorde dwarfs a biplane parked beneath its nose.

When Charles Lindbergh flew his plane, the *Spirit of St. Louis*, across the Atlantic in 1927, crowds on both sides of the ocean cheered in disbelief. He had made the 3,610-mile trip from New York to Paris in thirty-three hours and thirty minutes, the fastest transatlantic crossing up to that time. In a period when ocean liners were the normal mode of transportation across the ocean—a journey that lasted more than a week—such speed was almost unimaginable.

People soon got used to this rapid form of travel, however, and wanted to go even faster. So aircraft designers replaced propellers with jet engines. In 1958, thirty-one years after Lindbergh's historic flight, a Boeing 707 crossed the Atlantic in half the time taken by the *Spirit of St. Louis*.

Yet some dreamed of going still faster. Shortly after World War II, Captain Chuck Yeager of the U. S. Air Force piloted a military plane to 700 miles per hour, faster than the speed of sound. Why couldn't passenger planes fly as fast? Some engineers in England set about to design a plane that could carry 50 to 100 people at speeds of up to Mach 2—twice the speed of sound, roughly 1,350 miles per hour. A plane that flies faster than the speed of sound is known as a

You Have Flames! The Official Cockpit Transcript

Pilot: Prepare for takeoff . . . Is everyone ready?

Copilot: Yes.

Flight Engineer: Yes.

Air Traffic Control: Go . . .

Copilot: Watch out.

Air Traffic Control: Concorde . . . You have flames . . . You have flames behind you . . .

Flight Engineer: Breakdown engine two . . . Cut engine two.

Pilot: Warning, the airspeed indicator . . . the airspeed indicator . . . the airspeed indicator . . .

Air Traffic Control: It's burning badly, and I'm not sure it's coming from the engine . . . You have strong flames behind you . . . So, at your convenience, you have priority to land . . .

Copilot: The gear won't come up.

Pilot: Too late . . . No time, no . . .

From the transcript of the cockpit voice recorder aboard Air France Flight 4590

supersonic craft, while planes that fly slower than the speed of sound are called subsonic.

Supersonic Cooperation

At almost the same time, some companies in France also began working on a supersonic aircraft. For nearly three years, England and France toiled separately, each trying to be the first to produce a commercial plane that would break the sound barrier. The process of designing, building, and testing models was lengthy and expensive, however. Some engineers thought that the two nations could accomplish more together than they could by competing against each other.

So, in November 1962, England and France signed an agreement to build what they hoped would be the world's first supersonic transport, or SST. Soon after, the former Soviet Union and the United States also began SST programs, but they eventually abandoned them because of safety and economic problems. The Soviet Union actually built and flew the first nonmilitary supersonic transport, but it was too expensive and unsafe.

England and France decided to produce two prototypes—working models they could fine-tune until they had exactly the right design. The two countries agreed to share equally all costs and profits in a joint effort that would be led by British Aerospace and its French equivalent, Aerospatiale. They called their shared dream the Concorde, and it would take more than ten years of research and 5,000 hours of flight testing to make that dream a reality.

A Concorde jet under construction at an aircraft hangar in England

1

Bright Beginnings and Unforeseen Problems

In March and April of 1969, the two Concorde prototypes—one built for France, one for England—took to the air on their maiden voyages, witnessed by enthusiastic crowds of journalists, aircraft engineers, government officials, ordinary spectators, and millions of television viewers the world over. These successful test runs were followed by several publicity-generating trips to various countries, which were meant to create interest in the Concorde among passengers and airlines alike.

By 1972, the British-French partnership had the only supersonic passenger plane built for commercial use. It had cost $3.5 billion to develop the Concorde (the equivalent of $20 billion today), but investors thought they could make up that amount quickly by selling their planes to airlines all over the world. Those airlines, in turn, hoped to sell tickets to thousands of enthusiastic travelers, eager to take the fastest trip of their lives.

In 1972, airlines in six different countries had already placed early orders for at least seventy planes. With its streamlined design, its luxurious furnishings, and its promise of speed and comfort, the Concorde was a triumph of technology and style. It was also a symbol of international cooperation and a testament to European pride and elegance. The Concorde was a glamorous, jet-set dream for impatient businesspeople and pampered entertainers alike. In 1972, the Concorde looked like the premier transportation of the future.

Financial and Environmental Concerns

The first Concorde built for passenger service had barely rolled out of the factory before the glittering dream of supersonic flight began to fade, however. Even while being touted as the plane of the future, it quickly threatened to become a billion-dollar bust.

The first problem was economic. In the early 1970s, the entire world was hit by an oil crisis in which the supply of oil was greatly decreased while its price increased dramatically. The Concorde used an enormous amount of fuel: 5,638 gallons an hour. Because it

Tuesday, July 25

4:40 PM

Air France Concorde Flight 4590 is prepared for takeoff from runway 26R of Charles de Gaulle Airport outside Paris, France.

could not hold more than 100 passengers, it used one ton of fuel per passenger on each one-way flight across the ocean. Almost overnight, the Concorde became very expensive—too expensive for many airlines—to operate.

The second serious problem was the Concorde's limited range. The plane's seventeen fuel tanks were relatively small (holding a total of 31,569 gallons of fuel), allowing for roughly six hours of continuous flight. The Concorde could fly from Europe across the Atlantic Ocean to the United States, but it could not carry enough fuel to fly across the Pacific without landing to refuel. This ruled out any trips from the West Coast of the United States to Asia, a long-distance route that was becoming popular with business and vacation travelers but was a long, tiring journey in a regular jet airplane. The transatlantic route alone would not bring in enough income to make Concorde flights profitable for many airlines.

Environmental concerns posed a third problem. Ecologists worried that fuel emissions from the Concorde would damage the ozone, the layer around the earth that protects it from the sun's harmful ultraviolet rays. The plane flies higher than others and expels a gas into the air that breaks down ozone. Some people also worried that water vapor released in the plane's exhaust would create a permanent cloud cover at high altitudes, resulting in either a new ice age or a greenhouse effect, trapping heat at the earth's surface.

Finally, sonic booms—shock waves created when a plane reaches and passes the speed of sound—caused alarm in many communities that lay along the Concorde's flight paths. In England and the United States, people protested what they called "noise pollution" over their cities. As a result, a pilot had to slow the plane to subsonic speeds when flying over land, which undercut the plane's main selling point—its amazing swiftness. So the plane was restricted to flights over the Atlantic Ocean, limiting the number of customers who would find the Concorde useful.

In the 1970s, due to the energy crisis and a severe economic downturn, airlines were more interested in keeping costs down than increasing speed, and most passengers were more concerned about saving money on a ticket than saving time. The Boeing

A British Airways Concorde arrives at Brize Norton Airfield in Oxfordshire, England, after its first supersonic test flight since the fleet was grounded following the July 2000 crash.

Corporation had recently built a jumbo jet, the 747. It used only one-fourth of the fuel consumed by the Concorde, could fly much farther before refueling, and could carry four times as many passengers. All of this made it much less expensive to operate. As a result, the price of a ticket on a 747 flight was ten times less than on the Concorde.

Suddenly, the Concorde—expensive for airlines and passengers alike—did not make much sense. Nearly every airline canceled its orders for the Concorde. The only airlines that continued to support the supersonic plane were British Airways and Air France, based in the countries that had worked for so many years and spent so much money to build it. In the wake of all the canceled orders, the original plan to build 300 Concordes was abandoned, and only twenty were constructed. Manufacture of the planes stopped altogether in 1979.

Overcoming the Problems

If the Concorde was too expensive to attract lots of customers, it would have to rely instead on very wealthy ones—people who could afford to pay the $7,000 to $10,000 roundtrip fare necessary to make the planes profitable. So in their advertising, the airlines concentrated on two features of the flights designed to appeal to target customers: speed and luxury.

The plane's speed attracted some powerful businesspeople. To them, "time is money," and spending a few extra hours on a slower airplane might cost them valuable time they could instead devote to meetings, deal making, research, or other work. On a transatlantic Concorde flight, passengers can make up the time lost in travel: A flight that leaves London at 10:30 AM will—after passing through five time zones at the speed of sound—arrive in New York at 9:30 AM, one hour earlier than it took off!

Some wealthy customers were less concerned with speed than with luxury. The airlines made the cabins elegant, with plush leather seats and chic décor. They served gourmet meals on fine table linen and

Queen Elizabeth of England and test pilot Brian Trubshaw examine the interior of a Concorde at London's Heathrow Airport on July 3, 1972.

with silver cutlery: shrimp cocktail, Norwegian salmon, Russian caviar, fine cheeses, lobster, steak, pastries, champagne, and vintage wine. Private lounges for Concorde passengers waiting to board offered refreshments, drinks, newspapers, magazines, phones, and even a coat check. When the flights ended, passengers were given "thank you" gifts such as expensive crystal and fancy pens, and their checked luggage was delivered to them immediately.

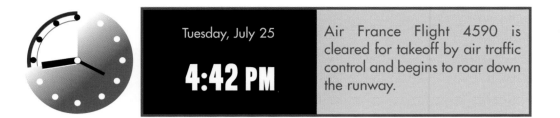

Tuesday, July 25

4:42 PM

Air France Flight 4590 is cleared for takeoff by air traffic control and begins to roar down the runway.

This advertising and promotion did the trick. In addition to wealthy corporate leaders, Arab sheiks, and prime ministers, many celebrities from all over the world chose to fly the Concorde, including musicians Elton John, Diana Ross, Mick Jagger, and Phil Collins; actors Robert Redford, Sean Connery, and Elizabeth Taylor; opera star Luciano Pavarotti; and boxer Mike Tyson. Prince Charles was a customer, and Queen Elizabeth of England preferred the Concorde to all other planes. Ex-Beatle Paul McCartney was a frequent flier as well. The Concorde did not become a common form of transportation as its designers had hoped, but it did become the luxury transport of the rich and famous. And that was enough to keep it airborne.

It was barely enough for the plane to make a profit, however. One by one, routes were closed as British Airways and Air France could not sell enough tickets on those routes to make money. Eventually, the only Concordes flying were once-a-day shuttles between New York and Paris and New York and London.

Safety Problems

In 2000, British Airways and Air France prided themselves on the Concorde's perfect safety record. In its thirty-year history, after tens of thousands of hours of flight, the Concorde had not had a single serious accident. No plane was inspected and tested as carefully or as often as the Concorde. Maintenance crews spent fourteen to eighteen hours on each supersonic jet for every hour the aircraft was in the air. Only the best pilots were allowed at the controls.

The planes were old, however, and had flown many miles. The fleet of British Concordes had spent more than 150,000 hours in the sky, while the French fleet had flown for more than 100,000 hours. Wear and tear were taking their toll on the planes, but replacement parts were difficult to obtain because the Concorde was such a uniquely designed machine; spare parts for subsonic jets—which were in large supply—would not work on the Concorde. The only way to get parts for repairs was to custom make them on demand or take them from Concordes that had been retired—planes that were just as old as the ones needing service.

Each year, as the planes got older, the fleets required more maintenance, and repairs were more difficult to make. Each year, preserving the Concorde's accident-free record seemed a little less assured.

The first major threat to the Concorde's clean safety record came in 1979. As an Air France Concorde took off from Washington, D.C., the captain felt a shudder and heard a bump. He guessed that a landing gear tire had blown but decided it could be fixed after arrival in Paris and would not prevent a safe landing. One passenger, aviation consultant Bill Lightfoot, also realized that something was wrong. He looked out the window and saw a hole in the plane's wing. None of the crew would listen to his frantic warnings until the copilot came to the cabin to calm him. "I held his head over to the window," Lightfoot said, and the plane returned to Washington. Two tires had burst, and the magnesium wheels had shattered; debris had damaged an engine, punctured three fuel tanks, and cut several hydraulic and electrical wires.

The wheels of the Concorde that crashed in Gonesse, France, were held in this warehouse. The French Bureau of Investigation of Accidents found that burst tires on both British Airways and Air France Concordes led to perforations in the aircrafts' fuel tanks six times prior to the July 2000 crash.

A month later, a second plane had a tire burst on takeoff. In 1987, five of the ten tires on an Air France Concorde burst as the plane touched down in New York. In all, at least nine incidents of tire failure were reported by 1993. Fortunately, none resulted in injury to passengers or crew members.

In addition to tire mishaps, engine problems plagued the Concorde. The jet's fuel tanks are located close to the engines. This poses a danger of explosion and fire if anything should go wrong with an engine. Prior to 2000, Concorde fuel tanks had been ruptured by bursting tires on six separate occasions. By 1997, the fleet had experienced twenty-one instances of engine failure. Some caused fires, but, luckily, none resulted in injury to people.

Einar Forberg: Catering Director

> "We are used to Concorde, but straight away we could tell the noise was wrong . . . It was too loud . . . It was hardly going up at all. There were flames from the number one engine and there were bits coming off . . . We could see it was in trouble, and it was obvious it was going to come down. We were just wondering how many people were on board and if any would live."
>
> **From Reuters**

Tires and engines were not the Concorde's only safety concerns. On at least four occasions, parts of the rudders fell from planes while in flight. In one instance, a plane lost a piece of its tail while cruising at high altitude. In one year alone, from August 1998 to July 1999, 130 incidents of mechanical or equipment failure of some kind were reported on Concorde planes. Once again, none of these incidents resulted in injuries.

On July 23, 2000, British Airways announced that it had found cracks in the wings of all seven of its Concordes. The next day, Air France found cracks in four of its six Concordes. These discoveries, alarming in themselves, would serve as a foreshadowing of something far worse to come. The Concorde's luck was about to run out.

2

Flight 4590

For many of the 100 passengers on Air France Flight 4590 from Paris to New York on July 25, 2000, this was going to be the adventure of a lifetime.

For years, school teachers Rolf and Doris Maldry had saved their money just for this trip. Photographer Christian Goetz and his wife were celebrating the fact that they had both overcome cancer. For Klaus and Margret Frentzen, it was to be the honeymoon they had never taken.

Most of the travelers had come from Germany to Charles de Gaulle Airport, just outside Paris. They were headed to New York to begin a two-week cruise aboard a luxury ocean liner, the MS *Deutschland*. They would sail leisurely through the Caribbean to Manta, Ecuador. Best of all, they would jet to New York at twice the speed of sound, on a plane chartered just for this trip—the world-famous Concorde.

"You Have Flames!"

The plane required a last-minute repair to its reverse thruster—the mechanism that helps a plane slow down upon landing. The repair took only thirty minutes, and the plane sat on the ground a little longer, waiting for some late baggage. Finally, at 3:58 PM, the crew requested the entire length of runway 26R for takeoff. The plane was only sixty-six minutes behind schedule, a delay that could easily be made up once the plane reached Mach 2.

A Japanese businessman took this photo of the flaming Concorde from inside another plane.

The Concorde was not the only aircraft to use runway 26R that day. A Continental DC-10 had taken off just minutes before Flight 4590. Charles de Gaulle air-port is the main airport serving Paris. As the eighth busiest air-port in the world, its terminals

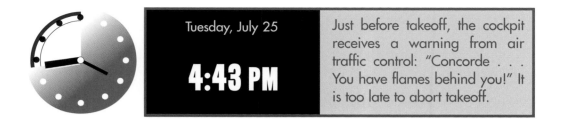

Tuesday, July 25

4:43 PM

Just before takeoff, the cockpit receives a warning from air traffic control: "Concorde . . . You have flames behind you!" It is too late to abort takeoff.

and runways are in constant use. The runways are usually inspected three times a day to make sure they are clear of debris. But on July 25, a fire drill had delayed the second routine runway check. When the Concorde taxied onto 26R, shortly after the DC-10 left, the runway had not been fully inspected for more than twelve hours.

According to a transcript of the cockpit voice recorder released by the French Bureau of Investigation of Accidents (the Bureau Enquêtes-Accidents, or BEA), at 4:42 PM, the ground controller authorized the crew to take off. Pilot Christian Marty asked, "Is everyone ready?"

The copilot and flight engineer both answered, "Yes."

Marty revved the engines and started the plane's rapid acceleration down the runway. "Up to 100 [knots]," he announced. "150." The engineer confirmed that all four engines were operating as expected. In less than a minute, the plane had accelerated to 200 knots, or 230 miles per hour.

As the Concorde streaked down the runway, what initially seemed like a routine takeoff suddenly went terribly wrong. At 4:43 PM, the controller's voice sounded over those of the pilot and copilot. "Concorde 4590, you have flames! You have flames behind you!"

It was true. Fire and smoke billowed from the back of the speeding airplane. Federal Express pilot Sid Hare was watching from a nearby hotel window. He told *Maclean's* magazine, "I knew it was in trouble . . . It was trailing flames 200 to 300 feet behind the airplane!"

An airport worker who had seen many Concordes take off told the *Washington Post* that the plane was louder than usual. "Black smoke was pouring out of the engines as it took off," she said. "I told myself that it wasn't possible it would take off if there was a problem."

At this point in the takeoff sequence, however, it wasn't possible to not take off. The plane had passed what pilots call the point of no return. It was going too fast for the crew to brake safely; there was simply not enough runway in front of them anymore. There was no choice but to continue and try to solve the problem in the air.

The flight engineer radioed the control tower that he had a breakdown in engine two. He was also having difficulty with engine one. The fire alarm sounded in the cockpit and, according the voice recorder transcripts, the engineer commanded, "Cut engine two." Copilot Jean Marcot saw that the plane was losing power. "The airspeed indicator! The airspeed indicator! The airspeed indicator!" he warned. He tried to retract the landing gear, but the wheels would not go up. The pilot tried to raise the plane's nose into the air and gain altitude so he could circle to a place where he could land. He was unable to do so. Alarms sounded, but they were unnecessary. The crew already knew that something was very wrong.

On the Ground

People on the ground also knew that the plane was in trouble. They could see one or both of its left engines on fire. They watched it struggle to climb but get no higher than 200 feet. They felt a gigantic wave of heat roar over their heads. They heard an explosion. They saw the plane turn and tilt and roll.

The air traffic controllers prepared for an emergency landing. Approaching planes were ordered to halt descent and enter a circling pattern, all runways were cleared of planes, and the Concorde was given permission to land on any of them. Traffic controllers alerted airport fire service to position its vehicles in order to be prepared for what would almost certainly be a fiery landing. Marty and Marcot, however, did not think they could slow the plane quickly enough to land at DeGaulle. "Too late," Marty answered the control tower. "No time." Marcot suggested Le Bourget, a smaller airport about thirty miles away, only a minute's flying time.

Rescuers stand near burning wreckage of Flight 4590 in Gonesse, France. The Concorde's pilot tried to avoid crashing in a populated area, but was unable to steer the burning aircraft away from a tourist hotel, the Hotelissimo.

Eid Assaad: Taxi Driver

"We watched it taking off when suddenly we saw a lot of smoke and flame coming out the back. There were hundreds of us there, and we were all saying, 'My God, that's Concorde!' It then turned sharply to the right. It looked like he wanted to try and land again. The captain tried to make it, the poor man . . . But they couldn't make it, and we saw the Concorde falling. There was a huge noise . . . That was the last we saw."

From Reuters

Sadly, the Concorde did not have a minute. Another explosion rocked the air, and engine one died. Marty apparently tried to steer the plane away from houses and other buildings toward an open field. It skittered across the tops of some trees as the pilot tried desperately to maintain control. Then the plane's nose pointed straight up, the craft rolled to the left, the nose spiraled downward, and the plane crashed violently into the Hotelissimo in the Paris suburb of Gonesse.

A column of fire erupted 300 feet into the air. Thick, black smoke clouded the sky for miles. "It was a sickening sight," said Hare, the Federal Express pilot who had witnessed the takeoff. "A huge fireball, like a mini atomic bomb."

Engulfed in the fireball were 113 people: 9 members of the flight crew, 100 passengers, and 4 bystanders on the ground. The time was 4:44 PM—only two minutes after takeoff.

3

Two Nations Mourn

The town of Gonesse is near Charles de Gaulle Airport. Thirty years ago, before the airport came to Paris, Gonesse was little more than a few streets and a handful of houses five miles outside the French capital. With the airport came jobs, and by 2000, the town grew to 22,000 people. Just about everyone in Gonesse either works at de Gaulle or is related to someone who does. "We live with the noise every day, every few minutes," one resident told the *Washington Post*. "But this . . . "

The Emergency Response

The fiery crash of the world's safest, most spectacular airplane jolted the little town. Hundreds of its citizens rushed to the blazing crater where the Hotelissimo once stood. But they could do little more than watch and weep. "The hotel was completely erased," one man told the *Washington Post*. "I knew there could be no survivors. There was nothing, nothing, absolutely nothing."

Within minutes of the crash, fire trucks, ambulances, paramedics, and police surrounded the wreckage. They moved the shaken onlookers 500 feet back from the site to keep them from becoming overcome by the toxic fumes of burning fuel, metal, and plastic. Firefighters directed their hoses on the flames. Then the police sealed the area off so they could begin their most important task: rescue operations.

It was soon clear, however, that the task was not one of rescue, but of recovery. A few people in the demolished hotel were injured, but 4 others and all 109 aboard the plane were dead. An amphitheater in the town was closed to the public and turned into a temporary morgue (a place where bodies are stored and identified).

The Mourning

France's president, Jacques Chirac, telephoned Germany's leader, Chancellor Gerhard Schroeder, with the sad news. The chancellor immediately canceled his vacation and ordered his country's flags lowered to half-staff. As reported in the *Washington Post*, he proclaimed, "Germany and France are united in their horror over the accident, in

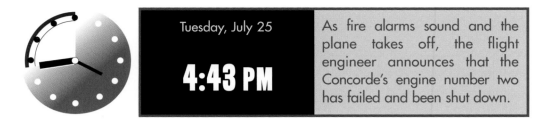

Tuesday, July 25

4:43 PM

As fire alarms sound and the plane takes off, the flight engineer announces that the Concorde's engine number two has failed and been shut down.

mourning for the victims and in sympathy for their families." The German Embassy in Paris sent people to the scene to identify the bodies of its citizens pulled from the smoldering wreckage.

Air France chartered a plane to bring families from Germany to Paris. Many of the relatives wanted to see the spot where the plane went down. More than 100 of them were taken in vans to Gonesse that afternoon.

Travel agent Peter Deilmann is surrounded by reporters as he enters a memorial service in Neustadt, northern Germany, for the victims of the Concorde crash. Most of the passengers on board Flight 4590 were Germans who had booked their voyages through Deilmann's travel agency.

Micheline Debruil: Gonesse Resident

"I was at my window, and I remember hearing a huge noise, much louder even than usual. Then there was smoke, so much smoke that I closed the window and ran inside, thinking it was the end of the world . . . But Concorde has got to fly again. It is a question of prestige for France."

From Reuters

On the same day that family members gathered in France, Chancellor Schroeder mourned in Germany. He interrupted the opening day festivities of the World's Fair in Hanover and turned the event into a memorial service. An estimated 350 mourners, including the entire German cabinet, attended. As reported in the *Washington Post*, Schroeder told the audience, "Germany is shaken. Germany is speechless."

The Investigation Begins

Meanwhile, the field where the Concorde came to a rest was alive with activity. Police closed off the site to all but airline investigators. Their job was to recover from the jumbled wreckage some information that would help explain the cause of the tragedy. They searched for the airplane's black boxes—fireproof instruments that record both the conversations in the cockpit and the readings on the plane's instruments. Investigators tried to identify every scrap of metal so they could later put the plane back together and discover what went wrong. It was like working with a 100,000-piece jigsaw puzzle.

An investigator inspects the remains of Flight 4590 at a hangar in Dugny, north of Paris. The crash killed ninety-six Germans, nine French crewmembers, two Danes, one American, and one Austrian.

For a full year the investigators searched the runway and crash site. They studied the photographs and videos that bystanders had taken of the plane's takeoff and crash. They combed the runway where the tragedy started and the rubble where it ended. They examined thousands of clues and talked to hundreds of people. For a year, they looked for anything that seemed out of place or unusual, anything at all that might explain how an aircraft with a thirty-year safety record was brought down in a few fiery seconds.

4

Who Is to Blame?

After the crash of Flight 4590, all Concorde planes were grounded. Authorities in both France and England revoked the planes' airworthiness certificates—the documents that declared the planes safe to fly. Both countries were eager to get their planes in the air again.

Though the Concordes were barely profitable to the airlines, they were still symbols of national achievement and pride. For the Concorde to fly again, the cause of the disaster had to be found and corrected. The BEA went to work.

Tuesday, July 25

4:44 PM

The flight crew tells air traffic control they can't make an emergency landing at Charles de Gaulle and will try the nearby Le Bourget Airport instead.

Clues and Theories

The first clues in the search for the cause of the crash were found in the debris on runway 26R. Pieces of tire—at least one of the Concorde's left undercarriage tires—littered the runway. One of these pieces was torn with a long gash. No debris from the wheels themselves or from any of the four engines was found, though a small part from one of the fuel tanks was discovered on the ground. Another item—a long, narrow metal strip—was found that did not belong to the Concorde.

The runway debris indicated that the tire had burst before the plane left the ground. Chunks of tire had been sucked into the engines, causing them to sputter. According to the black boxes, engine number one cut off and on repeatedly, and engine number two failed completely. The tire shards acted like bullets, piercing the engines and the fuel tanks, and resulting in a fuel leak. This leak ignited a deadly fire.

The safety experts revisited other incidents of Concorde tire failures that had occurred as far back as 1979. In several of those, engines or fuel tanks had been punctured by flying chunks of tires. The supersonic jet was especially prone to tire bursts because its extremely high takeoff and landing speeds caused great heat and stress on the tire rubber.

But what had caused the tire on Flight 4590 to blow apart—heat, stress, or that mysterious metal strip found on the runway? The BEA looked at the rip in the tire and the small piece of unidentified metal. If the supersonic jet had rolled over the metal strip at a high speed, the tire could have been slashed, setting in motion the chain of events that ended in the crash of the Concorde.

Investigators did not take long to identify the metal strip. It was a small plate called a wear strip that was supposed to be attached to the thrust reverser of an engine. Made of titanium metal, it was hard enough to slash a heavy tire. The BEA guessed that it had fallen from another plane, one that had used runway 26R

This sixteen-inch strip of metal was found on the runway at Charles de Gaulle Airport in Paris following the crash of Flight 4590. It came from a Continental Airlines DC-10 that took off from runway 26R shortly before the Concorde. Investigators believe the metal gashed a forward tire on the Concorde's left landing gear, triggering the chain of events that caused the supersonic plane to crash.

sometime before the Concorde. All the evidence pointed to the aircraft that had lifted off just minutes before the Concorde, a Continental Airlines DC-10.

Tuesday, July 25

4:44 PM

The Concorde crashes into the Hotelissimo in the Paris suburb of Gonesse less than two minutes after takeoff.

When BEA investigators examined Continental's DC-10, they saw that one wear strip was indeed missing. They noticed that the strip found on the runway was different from the other wear strips that were still attached to the plane; the one found on the runway was longer than the others, it was twisted, and a rivet was missing.

Continental Airlines initially admitted that the part had dropped from its plane. Investigators wanted to know why. The answer stunned them. Thrust reverser wear strips need to be replaced every once in a while, and this one was itself a replacement, attached to the plane just sixteen days before the ill-fated flight. The pattern of holes drilled in the strip where it would attach to the reverser was not the standard pattern, however. This particular wear strip had not been designed for the DC-10; simply put, it didn't fit the airplane properly.

Not only had the maintenance crew attached an ill-fitting wear strip on the Continental plane, but the crew also had neglected the properly installed wear strips that were still on the airplane. The BEA commented that the amount of wear on the remaining strips was "greatly in excess of the tolerance permitted by the manufacturer." All of the evidence pointed to poor maintenance by Continental Airlines.

Assigning Blame

When the BEA issued its preliminary report on the crash, it claimed that the piece of metal that fell from the DC-10 had set the Concorde disaster in motion, and was a result of "a lack of rigorous maintenance." Continental objected to this conclusion, claiming the following: The airport was responsible for clearing debris off of the runways; the Concorde had an unsafe design; and Continental had been unable to confirm that the wear strip came from its DC-10.

The report detailed other contributing factors, such as similar maintenance problems at Air France. It mentioned a spacer bar that had been left off the Concorde's undercarriage when it was serviced four days before the accident. The missing spacer bar may have made the Concorde veer to one side during takeoff, forcing the pilot to lift off before the plane was moving fast enough to stay airborne. A faulty repair of the plane's landing gear was also thought to have caused overheating during takeoff, possibly causing it to break apart and puncture the engines and fuel tank. According to the BEA, however, these were not main causes of the crash. The report laid the blame squarely on Continental and the wear strip.

Michelin executives introduce a new tire developed just for Concorde aircraft. The radial NZG (for Near Zero Growth) uses material designed to prevent ruptures like the one thought to have caused the jet's July 2000 crash.

Rebuilding the Concorde

Even before the BEA report was released, Air France and British Airways began working to regain airworthiness certificates for the Concorde. They contracted with Michelin to develop a tire that would withstand both the stress of high temperatures and contact with runway debris. Michelin gave them a radial tire it described as "almost indestructible." The airlines rebuilt the Concorde's fuel tanks, lining them with Kevlar, a material used in bulletproof vests. They believed that Kevlar-lined tanks would resist puncture and fuel leaks. Concorde engineers reinforced the wiring on the Concorde's undercarriage with steel to prevent sparks from flying and starting a fire. The plane's warning systems were also improved.

These changes were expensive. British Airways spent more than $24 million overhauling its fleet. But keeping the planes on the ground was expensive, too. Every month the jets did not fly, Air France lost the equivalent of $4.07 million and British Airways lost the equivalent of $9.64 million.

July 25, 2001, marked the one-year anniversary of the Concorde tragedy. It was a day of sadness and a day of hope. More than 250 relatives of those who had died in the crash traveled once more to de Gaulle

Conclusion

Airport. A marble and bronze memorial was unveiled in the garden of Air France's head-quarters. Engraved on the stone in French, German, and English were these simple words: "In memory of the 113 people who lost their lives in the Concorde AF 4590 disaster on July 25th, 2000."

Residents of Gonesse lay flowers at the site of the Concorde crash during a ceremony marking its first anniversary.

The relatives of those who died on July 25 went to Gonesse. Those who had come to the Paris suburb a year earlier remembered it as a field with the burnt remains of a once stately airliner. What they saw on this day was a concrete lot walled in by an iron fence and land still bearing scorch marks from the crash. The people of Gonesse had put wreaths on the ground in memory of the 113 victims, and flight attendants gave roses to family members. Air France staff around the world observed a minute of silence in honor of the dead.

Out of the Ashes

Although the day was one of sorrow in Gonesse, it was one of excitement in London. The week before, British Airways had tested one of its six refitted Concordes. The plane had soared over the Atlantic, reached supersonic speed, and flown for two and a half hours before landing to the cheers of many hopeful employees. Air France had made the required changes to only one of its five remaining Concordes, but the French airline planned to test it soon. The final BEA analysis of the crash had been issued the day before, and airline officials were confident that nothing in the report would keep their planes from receiving airworthiness certificates. Mike Bell, a British aviation official, told the Associated Press that, with all the improvements made to the Concordes, "There is less than a one in one billion chance of [a crash] happening again."

The Concorde Flies Again

Normal daily passenger service was restored on November 7, 2001, when an Air France Concorde with ninety-two passengers, including the French transport minister, Jean-Claude Gayssot, and Air France's chairman, Jean-Cyril Spinetta, flew from de Gaulle to New York City's

John F. Kennedy Airport in just under four hours. According to *The New York Times* Web site, Spinetta proclaimed, "This is the greatest tribute we can pay to the 113 people who lost their lives, and to whom I dedicate this flight." Within an hour, a British Airways Concorde also landed, carrying the British rock star Sting among its passengers. He told the Associated Press that he was "still excited about going on the Concorde after all

Captain Mike Bannister chats with rock star Sting aboard the Concorde on one of its first flights after the July 2000 crash.

these years. Flying at twice the speed of sound gives you a buzz." British prime minister Tony Blair flew out in the next Concorde to leave London, bound for Washington, D.C., and a meeting with U.S. president George W. Bush.

Ironically, the tragedy of Flight 4590 and its aftermath may have injected new life into the Concorde and helped insure its continued use for years to come. Before the accident, some people in the aviation industry had been concerned about the jet's safety. "This plane has been pushed to the limit," one pilot complained to the *Sydney Morning Herald*. "We've been living on the edge. I've had a feeling for some time that something could go badly wrong."

The long list of incidents of burst tires, rudder problems, and engine failures led to many complaints. In France, one pilot, speaking to the *Sydney Morning Herald*, compared keeping the planes in good working order to "watching twenty-five saucepans of milk being heated simultaneously on a giant stove." He said engineers were expected to perform miracles to fix the many problems on the planes.

For years the airlines ignored these complaints. They had an accident-free record and an attitude of "it hasn't really broken, so we don't need to fix it." But Flight 4590 changed all that. The wrenching tragedy forced the airlines to reexamine everything about the Concorde and give it a complete overhaul. They could no longer patch up problems but instead had to redesign major parts.

In facing up to and correcting their planes' flaws, British Airways and Air France have revitalized the Concorde, still the only supersonic passenger transport in use today. The dream of safe supersonic travel has been restored, though at a horrible price.

Glossary

airworthiness certificates Documents issued by government authorities that authorize planes to fly.

debris Pieces of trash or broken things.

knot Speed equal to one nautical mile per hour, about 1.15 mph.

Mach A measure of speed. Sound travels at Mach 1.

prototype A working model; a first attempt to build something.

shard A broken piece of a larger whole.

sonic boom Loud noise made by a moving object at the moment it reaches the speed of sound.

sound barrier The point at which an object travels at or beyond the speed of sound.

SST Supersonic transport; a plane that can travel at supersonic speed.

stratosphere The part of the sky that begins six miles above the surface of the earth.

subsonic Slower than the speed of sound.

supersonic Faster than the speed of sound.

thrust reverser A device on a plane's engine that helps the plane to brake.

undercarriage The landing gear of an aircraft.

For More Information

Organizations

BAE Systems (British Aerospace)
6 Carlton Gardens
London, UK SW1Y 5AD
Web site: http://www.baesystems.com

Bureau Enquêtes-Accidents (BEA)
Bureau of Investigation of Accidents
Bâtiment 153 Aéroport du Bourget
93350 Le Bourget, France
Web site: http://www.bea-fr.org/anglaise/index.htm

Federal Aviation Administration (FAA)
800 Independence Avenue SW
Washington, DC 20591
(202) 366-4000
Web site: http://www.faa.gov

Jane's Information Group
1340 Braddock Place, Suite 300
Alexandria, VA 22314-1657
(800) 824-0768
Web site: http://www.janes.com

Smithsonian National Air and Space Museum
7th and Independence Avenue SW
Washington, DC 20560
(202) 357-2700
Web site: http://www.nasm.edu

Web Sites

Due to the changing nature of Internet links, the Rosen Publishing
Group, Inc., has developed an online list of Web sites related to the
subject of this book. This site is updated regularly. Please use this
link to access the list:

http://www.rosenlinks.com/wds/crco/

For Further Reading

Bartelski, Jan. *Disasters in the Air: Mysterious Air Disasters Explained*. Shrewsbury, England: Airlife Publishing, Ltd., 2001.

Bingham, Caroline. *DK Big Book of Airplanes*. New York: Dorling Kindersley, 2001.

Coote, Roger. *Air Disasters*. New York: Thomson Learning, 1993.

Gesar, Aram, and J. Ott. *Jets: Airliners of the Golden Age*. St. Paul, MN: Motorbooks International, 1996.

Landau, Elaine. *Air Crashes*. New York: Franklin Watts, 2000.

Murdico, Suzanne J. *Concorde*. New York: Children's Press, 2001.

Reithmaier, L.W. *Mach 1 and Beyond: The Illustrated Guide to High-Speed Flight*. New York: McGraw-Hill Professional Publishing, 1994.

Bibliography

Blackburn, Al. *Aces Wild: The Race for MACH 1*. Wilmington, DE: Scholarly Resources, 1998.

Bowman, Martin W. *Classic Early Jetliners: 1958–1979*. St. Paul, MN: Motorbooks International, 2001.

Came, Barry. "Takeoff to Disaster." *Maclean's*, Aug. 7, 2000, p. 20.

CNN.com. "Concorde Fuel Tanks Burst 'Six Times.'" January 5, 2001. Retrieved November 2001 (http://www10.cnn.com/2001/WORLD/europe/france/01/05/concorde.report).

CNN.com. "Transcript: The Concorde's Final Two Minutes." September 1, 2000. Retrieved November 2001. (http://europe.cnn.com/2000/WORLD/europe/08/31/france.concorde.talk).

Concordesst.com. "Concorde." 2001. Retrieved November 2001 (http://www.concordesst.com).

Concordesst.com. "Accident News Archive." 2001. Retrieved November 2001 (http://www.concordesst.com/accident/archive.html). Includes news stories from Reuters and the Associated Press.

Drozdiak, William, and Charles Trueheart. "God, Where Were You in Paris?" *The Washington Post*, July 27, 2000, p. A19.

Drozdiak, William. "Tragic End to the Trip of a Lifetime." *The Washington Post*, July 26, 2000, p. A20.

Gaffney, Timothy R. *Air Safety: Preventing Future Disasters*. Berkeley Heights, NJ: Enslow, 1999.

Hallion, Richard P. *Supersonic Flight: Breaking the Sound Barrier and Beyond*. London, UK: Brasseys, Inc., 1997.

"Has Concorde Flown too Far?" *The Sydney Morning Herald*, July 31, 2000, p.A1.

Marshall Brain's How Stuff Works. "How Concordes Work." 1998–2001. Retrieved November 2001 (http://www.howstuffworks.com/concorde.htm).

The New York Times on the Web. "Concorde Passenger Flights Resume." November. 7, 2001. Retrieved November 2001 (http://www.nytimes.com/aponline/international/AP-Concordes-Return.html).

Owen, Kenneth. *Concorde and the Americans*. Washington, DC: Smithsonian Institution Press, 1997.

Trubshaw, Brian. *Concorde: The Inside Story*. Stroud, UK: Sutton Publishing, 1996.

Trueheart, Charles. "The Plane Climbed, Climbed . . . Then it Fell." *The Washington Post*, July 26, 2000, p. A19.

Index

About the Author

Ann Byers is a teacher, writer, and editor in California. She works with teenage moms. This is her sixth book.

Photo Credits

Cover, pp. 1, 18 © AFP/Corbis; pp. 4–5, 24 © Reuters NewMedia Inc./Corbis; p. 6 © James A. Sugar/Corbis; p. 9 © Hulton-Deutsch Collection/Corbis; pp. 13, 21, 28, 30, 33, 36, 38, 39 © AP/Wide World Photos; p. 15 © Bettmann/Corbis.

Series Design and Layout

Les Kanturek